D0467846

ABDO Publishing Company

BUGS!
Termites

Kristin Petrie

visit us at
www.abdopublishing.com

Published by ABDO Publishing Company, 8000 West 78th Street, Edina, Minnesota 55439.
Copyright © 2009 by Abdo Consulting Group, Inc. International copyrights reserved in all
countries. No part of this book may be reproduced in any form without written permission from the
publisher. The Checkerboard Library™ is a trademark and logo of ABDO Publishing Company.

Printed in the United States.

Cover Photo: Getty Images
Interior Photos: Alamy pp. 23, 25, 26; Andy Williams/CritterZone.com p. 19; Clemson
    University/Bugwood.org p. 24; Corbis pp. 9, 28; Getty Images pp. 1, 7, 15, 16; iStockphoto
    p. 12; Kim Taylor/Minden Pictures p. 19; Mitsuhiko Imamori/Minden Pictures p. 18; Peter
    Arnold pp. 11, 22; Photo Researchers pp. 17, 27; Scott Bauer/Bugwood.org pp. 5, 13; USDA
    Forest Service Archive/Bugwood.org p. 18; Whitney Cranshaw/Bugwood.org p. 21

Series Coordinator: BreAnn Rumsch
Editors: Megan M. Gunderson, BreAnn Rumsch
Art Direction & Cover Design: Neil Klinepier

Library of Congress Cataloging-in-Publication Data

Petrie, Kristin, 1970-
 Termites / Kristin Petrie.
     p. cm. -- (Bugs!)
 Includes index.
 ISBN 978-1-60453-071-1   41953307   11/09
 1. Termites--Juvenile literature. I. Title.

QL529.P48 2008
595.7'36--dc22

                              2008005927

Contents

Terrific Termites

Did you know there are insects out there that can eat your house? These teeny, tiny bugs can turn wooden homes into dust. To make matters worse, these hungry troublemakers are sneaky about their work.

Their munching usually starts deep inside wood. If left alone, they will eat until a building falls to the ground. What are these destructive insects? They are termites!

Many people think termites are pests. After all, who wouldn't be upset if their house were being eaten? Repairing termite damage can be costly.

Other people overlook the harm termites do. For example, **entomologists** are more interested in the ways termites work together. They are impressed by the **complex** homes termites build. These scientists are also astounded by this insect's amazing ability to survive.

Termites are impressive creatures. Many never see the light of day. However, their underground work has a big effect on the environment.

What Are They?

Termites are insects. Like all insects, they are from the class Insecta. Within this class, termites belong to the order Isoptera. **Entomologists** divide this order into six families. Within these six families, there are around 3,000 termite species.

Each species of termite has a two-word name called a binomial. A binomial combines the genus with a descriptive name, or epithet. For example, an eastern subterranean termite's binomial is *Reticulitermes flavipes*.

Like ants and bees, termites are social insects. They live in **colonies**. Some colonies have a few hundred individual termites. Others have as many as 7 million. Worldwide, there are billions of termites!

Termites are often called white ants. This name is due to the similar size and body features of termites and ants. In addition, termites and ants have some similar behaviors.

BUG BYTES

Isoptera comes from Greek words that mean "equal winged." Yet only a small percentage of termites has wings.

Is that bug you've spotted a termite or an ant? Look at its body shape! Ants have a waist, while termites do not.

THAT'S CLASSIFIED!

Scientists use a method called scientific classification to sort the world's living organisms into groups. Eight groups make up the basic classification system. In descending order, they are domain, kingdom, phylum, class, order, family, genus, and species.

The phrase "Dear King Philip, come out for goodness' sake!" may help you remember this order. The first letter of each word is a clue for each group.

Domain is the most basic group. Species is the most specific group. Members of a species share common characteristics. Yet, they are different from all other living things in at least one way.

Teamwork

A termite **colony** is divided into castes. A caste is a group of termites that performs specific tasks. There are three termite castes. They are reproductive termites, soldier termites, and worker termites.

Reproductive termites are responsible for growing the colony. They mate and produce eggs. Members of this caste include a king and a queen.

Soldier termites make up the next caste. They are responsible for protecting the rest of the colony and its nest. Some soldiers fight off predators with their jaws. They may also keep out invaders by blocking the nest's entrances.

Worker termites make up the final caste. These termites search for food to feed the entire colony. They also have another big job. Workers **digest** the food for all the other termites! Then, they place it directly into the mouths of other termites. Without this service, the entire colony would starve.

The worker caste is the largest in the **colony**. Because there are so many of these termites, they have extra jobs. For example, workers clean the nest of waste and other debris. They also care for the colony's young.

The queen relies on workers for many things, including food.

Body Parts

Have you been wondering how termites burrow through all that wood without getting hurt? The answer is protective armor! Like all insects, termites have an exoskeleton. The exoskeleton protects their insides. It also gives termites their body shape.

The termite's body is divided into three **segments**. These are the head, the thorax, and the abdomen. A termite's caste determines the size and shape of these parts.

The head segment looks the most different from caste to caste. Reproductive termites have round heads that feature compound eyes. Compound eyes have many lenses connected as one. Worker termites have larger round heads. The workers may or may not have eyes.

Soldier termites have the largest heads of all three castes. They do not have eyes, but their hard heads are still useful. In fact, soldiers sometimes use their heads to block the entrances to their nest.

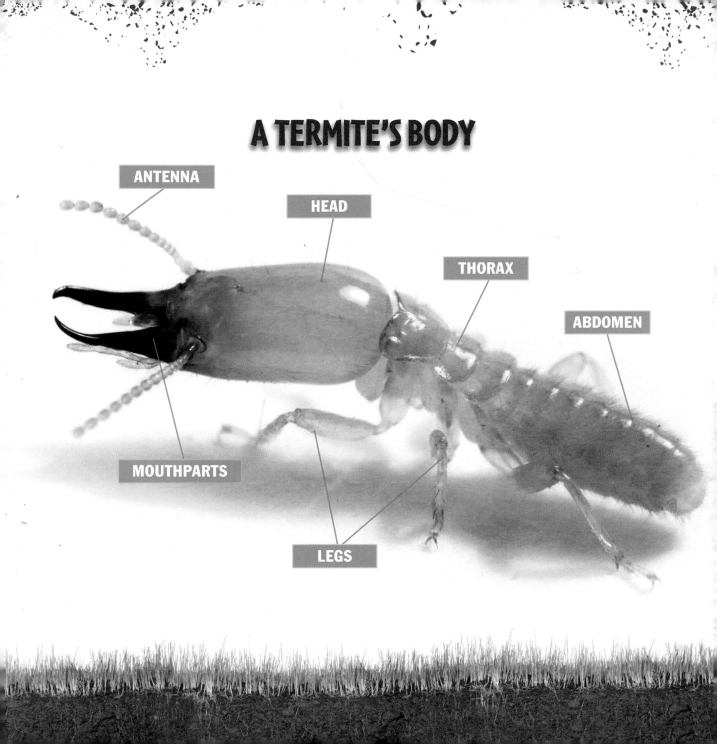

A TERMITE'S BODY

ANTENNA

HEAD

THORAX

ABDOMEN

MOUTHPARTS

LEGS

Another obvious difference among castes is the mouthparts. Worker termites have strong jaws called mandibles. These help them gather and chew tough foods. Reproductive termites have only small chewing mouthparts.

Workers are responsible for all the damage termites do to wood.

The shape and size of a soldier termite's mouthparts depends on its species. Some soldier termites have no jaws at all. Others have large, bladelike pincers. These big, sharp mouthparts stick out in front of the soldier's head. They make powerful weapons against enemies.

Termites from all three castes have two antennae on their heads. Antennae help termites communicate with one another. Termites do this by sending and receiving chemical messages called **pheromones**.

The thorax is the second **segment** of a termite's body. Every termite has six legs extending from its thorax. These quick little legs are a termite's main method of movement. A reproductive termite also has two sets of wings on its thorax. The other castes do not have wings.

Soldier termites are recognized for their large heads. Many are also noted for their large mandibles.

Beyond the termite's thorax is its abdomen. The abdomen is the longest body segment. That is because it houses many of the termite's **organs**. A queen termite's abdomen also houses her eggs.

The Inside Story

Inside a termite, important **organs** and body systems work together to keep its body moving. These systems help the termite survive in its **environment**.

Did you know that a termite does not breathe with lungs? Its respiratory system is very different from yours. Oxygen enters the termite's body through holes called spiracles. Inside, tubes called tracheae connect to the spiracles. These tubes carry oxygen throughout the termite's body.

Like most insects, a termite has an open circulatory system. This means blood flows freely throughout its body. Termite blood is called hemolymph. A termite's heart is a simple, long tube. The heart pumps hemolymph from one end of the termite's body to the other.

A simple brain and a **nerve** cord make up a termite's nervous system. Nerves extend from the cord throughout the termite's body. These nerves help control the termite's movements, senses, and organs.

Termites are hard workers! They depend on their body systems to keep them in tip-top shape.

Transformation

A new termite **colony** begins when reproductive male and female termites mate. These winged termites fly out of their nest. Then, they use **pheromones** to find a winged mate. During this activity, they are known as swarmers.

Once a male and a female find each other, they remove their wings. Then, they wander off in search of a good location for a new nest. There, they mate and begin the life cycle of their new colony. This male and female are the colony's king and queen.

When winged reproductive termites are ready to reproduce, they become attracted to light. This change guides them to exit the nest and find a mate.

BUG BYTES

In many insect orders, males do not remain with one female or their young. However, a termite king remains by the queen's side for his entire life span.

Many queen termites become so swollen with eggs they cannot move. For example, a Macrotermes subhyalinus *queen is known to reach 5.5 inches (14 cm) long and 1.4 inches (3.5 cm) wide. She may produce up to 30,000 eggs per day!*

A termite's life cycle is called incomplete **metamorphosis**. This life cycle has three stages. The first two are egg and nymph. Then, termites become either workers, soldiers, or reproductives.

After the king and queen mate, the queen termite's only job is to lay eggs. This job keeps her very busy! She stays still and produces eggs daily. Each time she lays eggs, hundreds of new termites begin their life cycle. The king and queen alone must care for the first baby termites. They will grow to become the **colony**'s first workers.

As the queen continues to lay eggs, worker termites take them to a safe place. The pearly white eggs hatch about two weeks later. These tiny termites are called nymphs.

While nymphs grow, worker termites feed and care for them. The nymphs grow quickly. In fact, they pop right out of their skin! Luckily, a larger skin has already formed below. This process is called molting.

During this phase, the nymphs develop into one of the three castes. Their development depends on the needs of the **colony**. If the colony needs to find food or build, nymphs turn into worker

LIFE CYCLE OF A TERMITE

EGG

NYMPH

termites. Are there a lot of enemies around? Extra soldiers are on the way!

The king and queen termites are the only termites in the **colony** that can reproduce. What if one of them dies? Then a nymph can molt into a reproductive termite. This ability secures the survival of the colony.

Life span in a termite colony varies. Many queen and king termites often live more than 20 to 30 years! However, worker and soldier termites work hard. So, they may live for only two to five years.

WORKER, SOLDIER, OR REPRODUCTIVE

Happy Homes

Where do termites live? Many termites like warm climates. However, these hardy creatures can also survive in cooler places. For example, about 40 termite species live in North America north of Mexico.

Some **entomologists** group termites according to two main features. These are their **habitat** and the type of home they build. When organized this way, there are four groups of termites. These groups are damp wood, dry wood, underground, and mound builder termites.

Damp wood termites live in and feast on damp wood. Rain forests and tropical locations are the perfect habitats for these insects. Dry wood termites live in and eat dry wood products. These tough termites need very little moisture to survive. Think deserts! Unfortunately, this also includes the wood in your house.

Next are underground termites. Most of these species build their nests below the earth's surface. Many of these sneaky critters never see the light of day!

Underground termites make cool mud tunnels. They lead to everything the termites need for survival. These tunnels can be very long and **complex**. They are used to find food. When a food source is found, the tunnels provide a fast route back home. They may also lead to other termite nests.

Some tropical termite species make their nests in trees. These nests are made with a hard material called carton. Carton is a mixture of soil, chewed wood or plant material, saliva, and waste. This material also constructs the tubes that lead away from the nest.

Mound builder termites are famous for their structures. They are found most often in Africa, Australia, Asia, and South America. By mixing soil with their **saliva**, these termites build towering mounds.

Inside, mounds have many different areas. These include the food storage areas, the nursery, and the king and queen's chamber. There are also vents that control the flow of air throughout the nest.

These skyscraper termite homes can reach 25 feet (8 m) in the air! People come from around the world to see them. They are natural tourist attractions.

Compass termites build tall, wedge-shaped mounds. They are called compass termites because their mounds always point north and south.

MASTER BUILDERS

Termites build homes designed to protect them from their environment. For example, African deserts can become extremely hot during the day. So, these termites build mounds that tower aboveground. The mounds commonly have chimneys. A chimney helps move air through the mound. This keeps the inside temperature cool.

In rain forests, a midafternoon rain shower could easily wash away bugs. So, termites in these locations may live inside trees. They build structures on the tree trunks that shed water like an umbrella.

Eating Wood

By now, you know what a termite's favorite food is. It's wood! In the wild, termites feed on trees and woody plants. In your house, they snack on doors, floors, and furniture.

All that tough food needs to pass through the termite's **digestive** system. First, food enters the foregut. From there,

Worker termites never rest from eating. It's no wonder they can turn a building to dust in no time at all!

it travels to the midgut. There, food is broken down and absorbed for energy. Cellulose, the main part of wood, is then digested in the hindgut. Finally, waste is released.

Can you imagine munching on a tree branch or a chair leg? Ouch! Do termites have steel throats? Are there chain saws in their stomachs? No way! In reality, termites cannot take full credit for this shocking feat.

BUG BYTES

Some scientists estimate that termites fart up to 165 million tons (150 million t) of methane gas each year! However, this is no laughing matter because methane is harmful to the planet.

Termites **digest** wood with the help of tiny organisms that live in their digestive systems. Yes, more bugs are inside of these bugs! Organisms such as bacteria and **protozoans** are responsible for breaking down cellulose.

FUNKY FOOD

Not all termites depend on bacteria and protozoans to help them digest wood. Some African mound-building colonies grow fungus gardens deep within the walls of their nests. These gardens help break down cellulose so the wood is digestible.

First, worker termites bring wood materials to the nest. Next, they chew up the wood to soften it. This soft material is then used to create a spongelike surface. White clumps of fungus grow on it. As the fungus spreads, it breaks down the cellulose. This leaves food the termites can eat.

Beware!

We know that termites love to eat wood. Do you know what loves to eat termites? Termites have a wide variety of predators. In the wild, bears are pretty happy to find termite nests. These treasure chests provide an endless supply of tasty termites.

Other termite lovers include birds, snakes, frogs, insects, and lizards. Less obvious predators include lions and chimpanzees. Humans may be the least obvious predators of all. In some **cultures**, people eat termites as part of their normal diet. Other people are just curious what fried termites taste like.

To catch a favorite snack, African chimpanzees insert a plant stem into a termite nest. When they pull the stem out, it is covered with termites!

How do termites protect themselves? Termites have a good warning system. When danger is present, some termites may run around or tap their heads on the ground. These actions produce vibrations. Other termites sense the vibrations in their legs. This tells them to run away!

To defend against attackers such as ants, soldier termites put up a good fight. Some have big, sharp mandibles made especially for biting. Other soldiers have a long snout from which they squirt a sticky chemical. It sends their enemies running!

Soldier termites guard the openings in their nest. A nasute soldier's head features a sharp, cone-shaped snout. From it, the termite can squirt a sticky, gluelike substance at intruders.

Termites and You

Many people study termites. Some are fascinated by termite **colonies** and caste systems. Others travel across the world to see termite mounds. These folks think termites are great insects!

However, most people do not like termites. This is usually the case when termites are eating their homes. To make matters worse, termites do their work in secret.

Their eating takes place deep within wooden structures. When the damage is finally noticeable, it may already be too late. In these cases, termites have become pests. They cause billions of dollars in damage to people's property every year.

On the other hand, termites in the wild are good for the **environment**. These nonstop eaters turn large wood pieces into smaller particles. These smaller particles decay easily. Rotten wood particles reenter the soil and help plants grow. Healthy plants put oxygen in our air and food in our stomachs.

Last, termites are a big food source for many creatures. They are a necessary part of the food chain. Fewer termites in homes would be nice. Yet no termites at all would spell trouble.

You may never see a termite up close. But you may see signs of its activity. When you do, remember what is happening beneath the surface. You can't help but admit these busy bugs are fascinating!

Professional termite inspectors are trained to locate areas in buildings where termite attacks are likely to occur. If termites are found, a specialist can treat the area. This will control the termite population and prevent future attacks.

Glossary

colony - a population of plants or animals in a certain place that belongs to a single species.

complex - having many parts, details, ideas, or functions.

culture - the customs, arts, and tools of a nation or people at a certain time.

digest - to break down food into substances small enough for the body to absorb. The process of digesting food is carried out by the digestive system.

entomologist - a scientist who studies insects.

environment - all the surroundings that affect the growth and well-being of a living thing.

habitat - a place where a living thing is naturally found.

metamorphosis - the process of change in the form and habits of some animals during development from an immature stage to an adult stage.

nerve - one of the stringy bands of nervous tissue that carries signals from the brain to other organs.

organ - a part of an animal or a plant that is composed of several kinds of tissues and that performs a specific function. The heart, liver, gallbladder, and intestines are organs of an animal.

pheromone - a chemical substance produced by an animal. It serves as a signal to other individuals of the same species to engage in some kind of behavior.

protozoan - a tiny, one-celled organism found in water, soil, plants, and animals.

saliva - a liquid produced by the body that keeps the mouth moist.

segment - any of the parts into which a thing is divided or naturally separates.

How Do You Say That?

antennae - an-TEH-nee
caste - KAST
entomologist - ehn-tuh-MAH-luh-jihst
hemolymph - HEE-muh-lihmf
Isoptera - eye-SAHP-tuh-ruh
metamorphosis - meh-tuh-MAWR-fuh-suhs
nymph - NIHMF
pheromone - FEHR-uh-mohn
tracheae - TRAY-kee-ee

Web Sites

To learn more about termites, visit ABDO Publishing Company on the World Wide Web at **www.abdopublishing.com**. Web sites about termites are featured on our Book Links page. These links are routinely monitored and updated to provide the most current information available.

Index